Love Laughs at Locksmiths: a comic opera: in two acts, etc. [By George Colman, the Younger.]

Anonymous, George Colman

The BiblioLife Network

This project was made possible in part by the BiblioLife Network (BLN), a project aimed at addressing some of the huge challenges facing book preservationists around the world. The BLN includes libraries, library networks, archives, subject matter experts, online communities and library service providers. We believe every book ever published should be available as a high-quality print reproduction; printed on- demand anywhere in the world. This insures the ongoing accessibility of the content and helps generate sustainable revenue for the libraries and organizations that work to preserve these important materials.

The following book is in the "public domain" and represents an authentic reproduction of the text as printed by the original publisher. While we have attempted to accurately maintain the integrity of the original work, there are sometimes problems with the original book or micro-film from which the books were digitized. This can result in minor errors in reproduction. Possible imperfections include missing and blurred pages, poor pictures, markings and other reproduction issues beyond our control. Because this work is culturally important, we have made it available as part of our commitment to protecting, preserving, and promoting the world's literature.

GUIDE TO FOLD-OUTS, MAPS and OVERSIZED IMAGES

In an online database, page images do not need to conform to the size restrictions found in a printed book. When converting these images back into a printed bound book, the page sizes are standardized in ways that maintain the detail of the original. For large images, such as fold-out maps, the original page image is split into two or more pages.

Guidelines used to determine the split of oversize pages:

• Some images are split vertically; large images require vertical and horizontal splits.
• For horizontal splits, the content is split left to right.
• For vertical splits, the content is split from top to bottom.
• For both vertical and horizontal splits, the image is processed from top left to bottom right.

LOVE LAUGHS AT LOCKSMITHS;

A Farce,

IN TWO ACTS.

———————

By GEORGE COLMAN, THE YOUNGER.

———————

LONDON:

Printed by D. Deans, Hart-street, Covent Garden;

For J. CAWTHORN, (Bookseller to Her Royal Highness the Princess
of Wales) No. 5, Catherine-street, Strand; and JAMES CAW-
THORN, British Library, No. 24, Cockspur-street.

———————

1808.

Price Two Shillings.

ADVERTISEMENT.

THE Farce of LOVE LAUGHS AT LOCKSMITHS is translated from a Parisian Comedy, in two acts, call'd *Une Folie;* written by *De J. N. Bouilly.*

Besides a total departure from the dialogue, in many instances, and various omissions, and curtailments, the French Piece is, altogether, very freely render'd into English.—The attempt, in short, has been to *naturalize* a very pleasant foreigner.

The reason for announcing this version, on its first representation in London, as the work of Arthur Griffinhoof, (a fictitious name) may be found in a prefatory Advertisement to " *The* " *Review; or, The Wags of Windsor,*" publish'd by Mr. CAWTHORN.

DRAMATIS PERSONÆ.

Vigil .... Mr. DENMAN.

Captain Beldare .... Mr. ELLISTON.

Risk .... Mr. MATHEWS.

Totterton .... Mr. GROVE.

Solomon Lob .... Mr. DE CAMP.

Grenadier .... Mr. HATTON.

Lydia .... Mrs. ATKINS.

SCENE—*London.*

LOVE LAUGHS AT LOCKSMITHS.

——————

ACT I.

SCENE I.—*A cross-way, in London; where several Streets intersect each other.*

On one side, in front, at the corner of a street, is Vigil's *house; all the windows of which have bars on the outside. Immediately over the door is an oval window, double grated, and two-thirds of it brick'd up. Opposite to* Vigil's *house is an Hotel.*

Enter Captain Beldare, *from the hotel, during the symphony of the following*

DUET.

Beld. *Why, where's the rascal? Risk! why Risk!*
Risk. (in the hotel) *I'm coming, captain.*
Beld.   *Zouns! be brisk!*
    The laziest knave I ever saw!
    'Tis day-light, puppy!
Risk. (enters gaping) *Yaw—aw—aw.*
    Whither so fast, that thus you scare one?
Beld. *To court a sweet, bewitching fair one.*
    Sweet God of love! thee I implore;
    Grant me the nymph whom I adore!
Risk. *Sweet God of sleep! thee I implore;*
    Grant me a bed, and let me snore!

Risk. *But, pray, who may the lady be?*
Beld.   *Apelles might be proud to draw her.*
Risk. *Is she so comely, then, to see?*
Beld.   *Upon my soul, I never saw her.*
    Sweet god of love, &c.
Risk. *Sweet god of sleep, &c.*

Risk. Never saw her! lord, sir, are you mad?

Beld. Certainly, you blockhead! Don't I tell you I'm in love?

Risk. Why, yes; but, to be mad for love before you see the woman!—Bless us! 'tis like getting drunk at a tavern, before the waiter has brought up a bottle.

Beld. Risk, come here.—Look at that corner building.   *(pointing to* VIGIL's *house.)*

Risk. What, with the bars outside all the windows?

Beld. Aye;—what do you think of it?

Risk. Think?—hem!—a Sheriff's Officer's.

Beld. 'Tis a celebrated painter's.

Risk. And glazier's?

Beld. Pshaw! an historical painter.

Risk. And you have just discover'd the history, sir, of his family?

Beld. Exactly so. He is guardian, or rather tyrant, to a young orphan, whom he locks up from the world, in the manner you observe.

          (pointing to the windows.)

Risk. I said 'twas a lock-up-house.

Beld. Listen. Although he lets nobody behold the original, many, I fancy, have seen the resemblance; for, in all his works, (and they are pretty numerous, here, in London) there is one peculiar character, one same beautiful expression, of a female face, ever to be observed.

Risk. Then you think, sir, that he takes her face for his model.

Beld. Just so.—Now what is your idea of me?

Risk. *(bowing)* That you have face enough, sir, to steal off with the prettiest face a painter ever had in his cabinet.

Beld. I shall try how far it may serve me, here:—but I shall have occasion, also, for a countenance to assist me, with a little more brass in it than I can boast.

Risk. (*bowing*) Dear sir, you are pleased to compliment; but command me.—I need not tell Captain Beldare, of the Grenadiers, that all the brass of his humble servant, Risk, is no more than the captain's own. And, now, pray, sir, how can my brass assist you?

Beld. Get me into the house.

Risk. Knock at the door, sir, and sit for your picture.

Beld Pooh! He doesn't paint portraits, I tell you;—only history.

Risk. Um—What's his name?

Beld. Vigil.

Risk. Vigil! oh dear! to the right about, Captain. Let's be off, directly.

Beld. Why, do you know any thing of him?

Risk. Know him? He's notorious! the most suspicious, lynx-eyed, peeping, peery, old pug of a painter, in Christendom.

Beld. (*carelessly*) No, is he, faith? I'm glad to hear it.

Risk. Glad!

Beld. To be sure;—it gives a double zest to the enterprise, you booby. Faint heart never won fair lady. Besides, she must hate old Virgil;—and a'n't I independent already,—with large expectations from a rich uncle? A'n't I a Captain of Grenadiers, with the *eclat* of having lately served against the enemy? and, a'n't I, with all the ardour of a true Englishman, panting to drub the enemy again, whenever they dare to attack our King and Country?

Risk. Bravo, sir! I believe it will do.

Beld. Do? to be sure it will! But, till Mars calls me, once more, abroad, I'll serve under

Cupid, at home. This is a fortress worth attacking; and here I commence my siege.

Risk. But are you quite sure, sir, the lady will like to be storm'd?

Beld. I think so. Yesterday she sang an air from that grated window. *(pointing to the oval window.)* I repeated the burden—she began again—her voice trembled—she recommenced, faulter'd, repeated, sigh'd—re——

Risk. Oh, the sweet little angel! say no more, sir: the castle is impregnable on this side;—but I'll reconnoitre on the other, and see where we can make a breach. I'll be back in a trice.

[*Exit, at the back of* VIGIL's *house.*

Beld. Now, if I could but, for a moment, catch her attention——

(The notes of a harp are heard from VI-GIL's *house.)*

Hark!

AIR.—LYDIA.

1st STANZA.

Hard is my lot, when youth is mine,
And joy should crown each rosy hour,
Within these gloomy walls to pine,
Still fetter'd by a tyrant's power.
Ye, who pity maids, like me,
This way bend, and set me free!

Re-enter RISK.

Risk. Sir! sir! sir!
Beld. Hush!

2d STANZA.

Must I, for ever, languish here,
A life of solitude to prove?
No; something whispers in my ear
That I was born for bliss and love.
Ye, who pity maids, like me,
This way bend, and set me free!

BELD. *and* RISK.

He, who pities maids, like thee,
This way bends, to set you free.

Risk. Bless her! she sings like a new one! and you and I weren't so much amiss, sir.

Beld. Now, tell me;—what have you discover'd?

Risk. A window, at the back of the house, without bars.

Beld. Without bars!

Risk. Only one story high; and that lower than usual from the ground.—There's only a green curtain, on the inside, to keep out the sun.

Beld. Vigil's painting room, depend on't.

Risk. It faces a bit of waste ground, to be let on a building lease,—where nobody passes;—so, we may plant our battery there, without fear of observation.

Beld. Excellent!

Risk. And, now, sir, if you succeed, do you mean to——

Beld. Hush! the door opens.

[VIGIL *comes from his house, follow'd by* TOTTERTON, *and double-locks the street-door after him.*]

Risk. That must be old Vigil, himself.

Beld. Away! away!

[*Exeunt* BELDARE, *and* RISK, *into the hotel.*

Vig. Totterton.

Tott. Here am I;—close at your heels.

Vig. Who was that officer, gliding from us, as we came out?

Tott. I can't tell:—but he looks plaguy suspicious.

Vig. Ay, ay, another butterfly, I warrant: fluttering about here, till he singes his wings, like the rest of them.

B

Tott. Oh, let you alone for smelling them out. Bless my soul, how you do nose them!

Vig. I can't be too circumspect: since my sister died, and left Lydia, her bewitching little devil of a cousin, under my care, I think, o'my conscience, the whole world has conspired to plague me.

Tott. Pshaw! 'tis love plagues you. Love for a green, kicking, frisky filly, of seventeen.— It will kill *me*.

Vig. Kill *you?*

Tott. Yes, it will. Have you not turn'd off all the servants, because you can trust nobody about her, but myself? A'n't I, who was, formerly, only your colour grinder, now your Jack-of-all-trades? A'n't I footman, porter, steward, cook, house-keeper, butler, scullion, and groom of the chambers?

[BELDARE *and* RISK *appear, listening, at a balcony of the Hotel.*]

Beld. Be attentive!—we may pick up some information.

Tott. Well, I must hobble off, now, after Levi Kaiserman, the Jew picture-dealer, from Germany.

Beld. (*aside to* RISK) Levi Kaiserman. Mark that.

Vig. That's right. He wrote me word, by the last post, that he should arrive, yesternight, in London.

Tott. Spread Eagle, Gracechurch-street.

Vig. Just so. Now you'll wait till he gets up, Totterton, then bring him, yourself, to my painting room. *Yourself*, remember.—No mistakes, now.

Tott. Mistakes! pshaw! I'm deep! I haven't made a blunder these sixty years. (*going*) Levi Kaiserman—what sort of a man is he?

Vig. I never saw him.

Tott. Umph! what age?

Vig. Oh, not very young:—about forty.

Tott. Forty? why, that's quite a boy; *(going)* but we shall be both from home at the same time. That's mighty wrong—Miss Lydia may——

Vig. No, no; she's in bed, and fast asleep. I knew I should be obliged to go to Somerset House, early to day, to look at the effect of my new picture, in the Exhibition; which is to open to-day;—so, what do you think I did?

Tott. What?

Vig. Kept her up, quarrelling, till five o'clock this morning: so, she's tired out, and wont 'wake till I come back. Ha! ha! wise! wasn't it?

Tott. Ha! ha! why, you are as cunning as—

Vig. I know what I am at.

> [*At this moment, a letter is seen descending, against the wall, from the oval window of* VIGIL's *house, attach'd to several ribbands, knotted together, like the links in a chain.*]

Vig. *(continuing his conversation)* Now, Totterton, you are a trusty old fellow; but what a pity it is, that your extreme old age disables you from serving me so much as——

Tott. My extreme old age!

Vig. Yes;—you are getting hard of hearing; and your eye-sight grows weaker every day: *(here* TOTTERTON *perceives the ribbands)* for which reason, you know, my old boy, I have sent for your nephew, from Yorkshire, to assist us. He's too great a bumpkin to fear any thing from his——

Tott. *(nettled)* And, so, my eye-sight gets weaker every day?

Vig. Well, well;—I didn't mean to affront you.

Tott. (keeping his eyes on the letter which is gradually descending) Why, to hear you talk, a body would think I was deaf and blind.

Vig. I didn't, exactly, say that.

Tott. And you are the only person that sees every thing, to be sure!

Vig. What do you mean?

Tott. Yes, you are the only person;—you, who think that your ward is fast asleep; while——

Vig. While what?

Tott. While what? why, while she is sending letters, post-free, by the first-floor mail. *(pointing to the letter, which is now three feet from the ground)* Look'ee there!

Vig. Zouns!

Risk. Oh the devil, sir! that was for us!

> (*aside, to* BELDARE.)

> [BELDARE *and* RISK *go from the balcony of the hotel.*]

Tott. Now who's the blindest of us two, I should like to know?

Vig. Hold your tongue.—Let us untie it, softly; and she will think it is come to hand, just as she intended. *(takes the letter)* For that rake helly officer, I'll lay my life. How the plague she could have managed from that window, to—but we shall see. *(breaking the seal.)*

> [BELDARE *steals out of the hotel, with* RISK.

Beld. Let us listen.

> [*They cross to the opposite side, and get, at a small distance, behind* VIGIL *and* TOT- TERTON.]

Vig. (coming forward, reading) " The in- " terest you appear to take in my fate, gives me " courage to convey this letter to you. I shall " lower it by a chain of ribbands, to which

" you may tie your answer; and I can pull it
" up."

       [BELDARE *pulls out his pocket-book, tears a*
         leaf from it, takes his pencil, and prepares
         to write.]

Vig. (reading) " Let me know your name.
(BELD. *writes*) " Your name—and your"—
'tis scrawl'd in pencil; and in such a cursed
hurry, I can hardly——

Tott. (who puts on his spectacles, and reads
over VIGIL's *shoulder.*) " And your designs."—

Vig. (continuing) Aye—" Your designs;
" and what I have to hope."

          [BELDARE *writes again.*
" I am confined by the bolts and bars of—of—"

Tott. (reading) " Of an old fool."—Ha!
ha! come, now, that's well enough.

Vig. Well enough, you blockhead! (*going*
on) " He is a perfect Cerberus; but I think he
" may be deceived."—Aye, that remains to be
proved.

Tott. Come; go on.

Vig. (proceeding) " My father died in the
" field of honour; I am seventeen years of age;
" with a fortune, and a figure which, I think,
" is not despicable. I have a good deal of gid-
" diness, of which I forewarn you:"—That you
have, with a devil to it!—" but an incessant
" flow of spirits, and, above all, a good heart:
" which I offer, with my hand, to him, who
" will rescue me from my present bondage.—
" Lydia."

Beld. Charming girl!

       [BELDARE *and* RISK *get nearer to* VIGIL
         and TOTTERTON, *and listen with the ut-*
         most attention.]

Vig. Now for the postscript. " Every
" morning, these ribbands may communicate

" our mutual thoughts, and plans.—Tie your
" answer to them, directly." (BELDARE *gives
the note he has written, on the leaf of his pocket-
book, to* RISK; *who ties it to the ribbands.*)
" And give me a sign by"——Stay, what's
this? Aye—" give me a sign by clapping your
" hands together, only once, when I may draw
" it up, without fear of discovery."—Now,
there's a Jezabel! (*remains pondering, with his
eyes fix'd on the letter.*)

    Risk. 'Tis impossible to give the signal, sir,
without their hearing us.

    Beld. Hush!

    Vig. What the devil am I to do with this
gipsy, Totterton?

    Tott. Keep her close still. Straw, and a
dark room.

    Vig. I cou'dn't be so cruel to such a sweet
creature, Totterton.

    Tott. I would.

    Vig. No, you wou'dn't.

    Tott. I would—and that's flat.

      [*Striking his hands together sharply. On* TOT-
        TERTON's *clapping his hands together,* BEL-
        DARE's *letter is, instantly, drawn up, to the
        oval window, and disappears.*]

    Risk. She has it, sir, she has it!

    Beld. In, in, in!

        [BELDARE *and* RISK *run into the hotel.*

    Vig. This must have been for that eves drop-
ping officer, who went into the hotel, and—
(*looks round*) Eh? egad, she has drawn up the
ribbands! and thinks, I warrant, to find an answer at the end of them! ha! ha! odsbobs! I
have bamboozled her finely! Totterton!

    Tott. Eh?

    Vig. Get you to Lydia's apartment, directly.
Lock all the doors; especially that that leads

to the balcony: and keep sentry, till I come back.

Tott. Then I mustn't go after my nephew. He's at the Bull and Mouth, by this time;—popp'd out of the York flying machine.

Vig. Pshaw! time enough for him. Besides, you know, he has our direction.—Now, get in; and don't let a single soul enter the house.

Tott. If Levi Kaiserman, the picture dealer, shou'd call——

Vig. Don't admit him;—it may be a trick. —Zouns! why are you so dull? not a creature, except yourself, (paticularly a male creature) shall be under my roof.

Tott. Well, well;—any thing to please you. —I'll go and chuck the tom-cat out of the garret window. [*Exit, into the house.*

Vig. And now, my gay blade of an officer, if you chuse to enter the lists with me, we'll have a trial of skill, that's all.—But 'tis getting late; I must be off to Somerset House. [*Exit.*

[*As* Vigil *goes out,* Risk *peeps from the door of the hotel.*]

Risk. There he goes! in the direct road to the Strand. You may come out, sir.

Enter Beldare, *drest as a German Jew, from the hotel.*

Beld. Having this masquerade dress by me, was lucky.—Don't you tinksh now, I looksh like de Shew, dat vash bring de choicesht pictures from Yarmany? (*mimicking the Jewish dialect.*)

Risk. And do you think, sir, you can impose yourfelf on him as Levi Kaiserman, the picture dealer, he expects from abroad?

Beld. At least, I'll attempt it. I'll be before

him at the Exhibition room.—The porter, there, is an old servant of my uncle's, and will let me into the place, where they are hanging the pictures. Vigil shall find me poring in raptures over one of his own productions.—Then I'll introduce myself as Levi Kaiserman, and—but I lose time.—Risk, be vigilant. (*going in haste, and forgetting his disguise.*)

Risk. But sir, sir! that air, and that dress, will never agree, in the street. You'll be discover'd.

Beld. Zouns! that's true, I had forgot, and should have spoil'd all. (*altering his gait, and manner*) You shay mighty true. The Shew vash shtupid dog, dat vash not know how to keep up his character.   [*Exit.*

Risk. And the Christian is a silly dog that runs mad for a woman he never saw in his life. Am I a fool? Hum—I think not. Then, why do I aid and abet a madman? Why to bring grist to my mill. When I have made up a purse, I'll retire, take a farm, and marry a Pomona; stick pigs, stump in the mud, buy bullocks, swill ale, and bully ploughboys.

SONG.—Risk.

Oh! when my farm is taken,
How delightful 'twill be o'er my acres to stump!
Then I'll marry a dairy-maid, jolly and plump,
But she sha'n't be as fat as my bacon.
I'll hire a lout to wield the flail;
Small beer shall serve the bumpkin;
Whilst I, with guzzling home-brew'd ale,
Grow rounder than a pumpkin.

I'll have hogs, dogs, cows, sows,
Turkies, ducks, and barley-mows;
Harrows, ganders, bullocks, ploughs;
  And I'll dazzle the country gabies.
    I'll get a bull,—I'll get a cart,
    I'll get the Farmers' Guide by heart;
And I'll get a dozen babies.
     Then I'll pet my dogs,
     I'll fat my hogs,
     I'll milk my cows,
     I'll salt my sows,
     I'll run my rigs,
     I'll stick my pigs,
     I'll roast my lambs,
     I'll mend my dams,
     I'll wet my knife,
      I'll kill my sheep,
     I'll kiss my wife,
      I'll go to sleep,
All when my farm is taken.

II.

I'll drink just double each Saturday night,
Sitting up, with my spouse, by candle-light,
  For I need not rise early on Sunday:
Then I'll prate to my lovee, of clover and barns,
While the dear little children's stockings she darns,
  That must go to the wash, on Monday.
On Sunday to church;—beef and pudding, at one;
    Then, the evening to spend,
    I'll get drunk with a friend,
Reel to bed, and, on Monday, be up with the sun.
  But, on Monday, my bed forsaking,
  Oh! how my nob will be aching!
    With my eyes, stiff and red,
    Sunk deep in my head,
I shall look as old as Methusalem!
    While the curst noises round me
    Will so confound me,
I shall wish the farm at Jerusalem.
  For, there, the pigs will be squeaking,
  The waggon-wheels creaking,

c

Ducks quacking,
Cart-whips cracking,
Turkies gobbling,
Carters squabbling,
Rooks cawing,
Ploughboys jawing,
Horses neighing,
Donkies braying,
Cocks crowing,
Oxen lowing ;—
Dogs bark,
Noah's Ark!
Gobble, wobble—weke—caw—caw,
Grunt—bow, wow—quack—moo—ee—aw!
All when my farm is taken.

[Exit, into hotel

Enter VIGIL, *and* BELDARE, *as* LEVI KAISERMAN.

Vigil. Our meeting, in the Exhibition room, was very fortunate, indeed, Mr. Kaiserman.

Beld. Yesh, it vash fall out mighty lucky.

Vigil. I am vastly happy to be personally known to you, at last. 'Tis to your good offices, you know, Mr. Kaiserman, that I owe the success of my pictures, in Germany.

Beld. No such ting, as I hope to be shaved: but you are sho modesht. Ah! dat ish sho like de great genius to be modesht. Blesh my soul! vat a sharming piece you vash shend to de Exhibition, dish morning!

Vigil. What, my Danaë? I thought it seem'd to strike you.

Beld. I declare, I vash ravish'd.—De execution vash sho capital!—de colouring sho chaste! —de—but vereabouts ish your house?

Vigil. (*pointing*) Oh, here, hard by.—Didn't you like that effect in stretching out the arms? something uncommon, to our school of painting, there; eh?

Beld. Vashtly uncommon ;—it ish so natural.

Vigil. And, were you pleased with my blue cloud ?

Beld. Pleash'd ! I protesht, if it had been black, I should have hoishted my umbrella. Den de shower of gold :—oh, dat ish fine !

Vigil. I was sure you'd approve of the shower of gold :—I don't know a Jew that wouldn't.

(aside.)

Beld. Come, take me in mit you to your home :—ve can't talk so well upon de shtreet.

Vigil. (*going towards the house, then stopping*) Well, well,—by the bye, how did you contrive to get admitted, so early, at Somerset House ?

Beld. I was a foreign artisht, you know.—

Vigil. Oh, true.

Beld. Sho I vash curious to shee de English school, and—but, come into your housh, and shew me your worksh.

Vigil. (*aside*) He is devilish pressing to get in ;—I don't half like it.

Beld. (*aside*) He hesitates.

Vigil. (*aside*) Zouns ! if this should not be Levi Kaiserman, after all !—I'll sound him.— (*to him*) You made an excellent bargain for me, abroad, in the sale of my Cassandra.

Beld. Oh, curse Cassandra ! (*aside*) Yesh, dat vash a mashter-piece.

Vigil. The purchaser, I think, was, was— pshaw ! I can't tell his name, now, for the soul of me !

Beld. Upon my soul, no more can I ! *(aside.)*

Vigil. Wasn't it the grand Duke of—of— ?

Beld. Of Bavaria.

Vigil. Aye—the Duke of Bavaria.—And to whom did I sell my Proserpine ?

Beld. Oh, Proserpine—I vash shell her to de Archbishop of Cologne.

Vigil. No; come, come,—not to him neither.

Beld. (*disconcerted*) Eh! vy not?

Vigil. Why, she was without drapery;—and to an archbishop! pooh! hang it! you're joking.

Beld. (*aside*) Oh, the devil!—His eminence vash scruple, at first; but de painting vash sho entishing, he couldn't reshist.

Vigil. And what did he give?

Beld. Ten thousand florins.

Vigil. Which you have brought for me.

Beld. No;—payable at four months.—Oh, you need not be alarm'd.—'Tish as good as de Bank.

Vigil. Oh, I'm not uneasy.—And, now, Mr. ——hem——Mr. Kaiserman, let me ask your opinion of a picture I have in my head.

Beld. Vat ish it?

Vigil. It consists of two figures. The first is an old painter; quick and cunning;—a sly fox of some fifty; who is reported to secure a young beauty, under lock and key, whose features serve him as a model in his works.—Here he stands.

Beld. (*aside*) What does he drive at?

Vigil. The second figure, is a gay stripling, with a plaguy air of intrigue. I have the model of *him* too. Now, the younker, to humbug the artist, takes the disguise of a Jew picture-dealer; but, the old boy, accustom'd to make greenhorns betray themselves, talks to him of a Cassandra he *never sketch'd*, and a Proserpine he *never painted.* How do you like the subject?

Beld. (*aside*) I wish it were upon canvass, and you were obliged to eat it, for breakfast.

Vigil. (*knocks at his door*) Well, now, upon

my word, you did it very well. I declare I
vash ravish'd! de execution vash sho capital!

(mimicking.)

Beld. Zouns! sir! I——

Vigil. Nay, nay, don't be mortified; for you
deceived even me, at first; and so I'll give you a
piece of advice:—never appear too eager to get
into the house; for that discovers you; and, pray,
pray, for the sake of *decorum*, when you have
another Proserpine to dispose of, don't " shell
her to the Archbishop Cologne."

[Exit, into his house.

Enter RISK, from the Hotel.

Risk. Well, sir, how goes on the war?

Beld. Countermined, and blown to the devil!

[Pulls off his false beard, and wig.]

Risk. I told you how it would be, sir. We
had better raise the siege, at once.

Beld. Hang it! I don't like beating a retreat.
Lydia, I am sure, must be charming.

(they talk apart.)

Enter SOLOMON LOB, from the top of the Stage,
with a canvass travelling sack at his back; two
letters in his hand, and a couple of small bundles
under his arms.

Lob. I'se sure this Lunnun Town's a hugeous
place!—aye,—and a bonny place, too. How the
streets, somehow, do grow out o'yan another!

Beld. After her letter, and my answer, it
would be paltry, unmanly, to abandon her. I'm
determined to get into the house;—but how to
find my way—!

Lob. Wauns, sir, I wish you'd be so kind to
put me into mine like;—for I'se lost it, outright,
I's sure.

Beld. Pshaw! go to the devil!

Lob. I isn't a Lunnuner, sir !—I doan't know that road.

Risk. What's the name of the street you want to find?

Lob. Neame ? why my uncle's master's.

Risk. And who is your uncle's master ?

Lob. He ! he ! I thought every fool i Lunnun know'd he.—Mr. Vigil, the noted Limner.

Beld. Mr. Vigil !

Lob. Aye ; I ax'd for un, as I coom'd alang, at sign o' Green Man :—I thought he might ha' painted it.

Beld. And, what do you want with Mr. Vigil, friend?

Lob. What do I want? what do I want wi my own uncle, there ?—who do grind all his stuff for un, to make sham men and women.

Risk. (*aside*) Here's a discovery, sir !

Lob. Uncle being old, and stupid gone, and a bit fondish, he sent for me fra' Tadcaster, to help his wits, and gi'un condolation ; for I be counted to have more parts nor all our family tied up in a bunch.

Beld. Tadcaster, in Yorkshire?

Lob. Aye ; neighbours of our town calls I the *Genus*.

Risk. (*aside*) And a damn'd queer *Genus* you are !

Beld. What's your name, friend?

Lob. Solomon Lob, sir.

Beld. (*affecting to start*) Is it possible ?

Lob Doan't te jump ;—but I *is* Solomon ;—I's sure I is ;—wauns ! now, wha knows but thou is Mr. Vigil, his sen !

Beld. I am the very man.

Lob. Well, dang me, somehow, if I didn't think so ! I be noted, as our Parson do say, for guessing at volks, instinkingly. Well, sir, and how be uncle, Totterton? Ods flesh, I han't ha' seen un sin I first went to plough.

Risk. Your uncle—hem—your uncle is just gone out; but we expect him home, directly.

Lob. Dost thee know uncle, too?

Risk. Yes;—I (like him) am Mr. Vigil's domestick.

Lob. A dumb stick?

Risk. Aye;—your uncle's fellow servant.

Lob. Be you, indeed! Oh, sir, (*to* BELDARE) I ha' summut for you, in this here little bit bag.

[*taking a small bag from his pocket, and giving it to* BELDARE.]

Beld, What's in it?

Lob. Golden guineas, by gum! Parson ha' sent 'em, for the picture you painted, for our church. Here be his letter to 'ee, sir,—explaining the rights on't. (*gives the letter.*)

Beld. Yes, yes; I see 'tis for me.

(*reading the address.*)

Lob. Parson be getting on i th' world, I assure ye, sir.

Beld. I'm happy to hear it.

Lob. He married his sister, last week, sir, to our rich hump-back'd letter-carrier; and, considering miss were nigh fifty, and bandy, t'were reckon'd a tightish match.

Beld. And what's that other letter in your hand?

Lob. For uncle Totterton.—Look at un, sir. (*gives it*) It do come from his loving sister, Margery; my mother, sir. Robin Rawbones, our blacksmith, wrote un for her.—Sin father died, Robin ha' been main comfortable to mother, and ha' done most of her odd jobs.

Beld. His sister, Margery—Robin Rawbones. —(*looks significantly at* RISK) Aye, Totterton has mention'd them to me, very often. I'll give

this letter to your uncle myself.   Let us get him away.   (*aside to* RISK.)
    [LOB, *taking up the bundles, which, during the scene, he has put on the ground.*]

Lob. I do suppose I be to go in, now, sir, and bide in your house.

Beld. To be sure.   How shall we parry that?
                                            (*aside, to* RISK.)

Risk. (*helping* LOB *with the bundles*) Zouns! fellow servant, what a deal of luggage you have brought up to London.

Lob. Pooh! this be nowt, mun.   Mother ha' sent I up, well rigg'd.   I ba' left portmantle, wi' all my best clothes, at Bull and Mouth, where we put up, wi' the coach.

Risk. At the Bull and Mouth? why, you'll be plunder'd!

Lob. (*frighten'd*) Noa! why, wauns, mun, ben't 'em safe?

Risk. Safe! run back, ready to break your neck, or you'll never see 'em again.

Lob. I wool.   Oh Lord! mother told I this ware a tricking town, sure enow.   Which way mun I——

Beld. When you come back,—look ye,—that is my house: (*pointing to the hotel*) you'll be sure to remember it.

Lob. Aye, sir—which is 'tway?—Oh, my poor portmantle!

Risk. Down this street—then to your right— then to your left,—thro' Pimlico, into Holborn, —turn short out of Pall Mall, into Finsbury Square; then any body will direct you. Run!

Lob. Wauns! it be hard to find.

Risk. Quick! quick!

Lob. I wool;—first turning to the—oh dear! Pall Mall Square, and—oh, my poor portmantle!   [*Exit, running, leaving his bundles.*

Beld. Now, Risk, be active.

Risk. I know what to do, sir   Here's a suit of the bumpkin's in the bundle; I'll help myself on with it, and that shall help me into Vigil's house, in a minute.

Beld. Here—take the letters, and the money—they will be your credentials;—but, can you speak the dialect?

Risk. Never fear. I'm Yorkshire myself, sir.

Beld. Indeed!

Risk. Lord, sir, you might have known that, by my modesty.

Beld. But, despatch;—get in doors, and prepare yourself;—help me off with my dress,—for I am heartily sick of it. (*throwing it off*) In the mean time, I'll keep watch here for honest Solomon; and, when he returns, I'll take him into our hotel, as Vigil's residence.

Risk. And when I am really in Mr. Vigil's, sir, do you take your post at the back of the house;—the weakest part of the fortress, which I have discover'd; and wait for my signal for getting you into the citadel.—Now for it! In three minutes I'll be Solomon Lob.

[*Exit, into the hotel.*

Beld. Once more, victory leans on my side.—And now, master Vigil, spite of all your cunning, I'll prove that youth, and love, will always get the better of age, and caution.

SONG.—BELDARE.

Ruddy Damon, sighing, said,
  " Let us, dearest Phillis, marry;"
Phillis smiled, but shook her head,—
  " Parents tell us we must tarry."

D

Still did amorous Damon press,
'Till to church they slipp'd away;
Age said " no;" but Youth said " yes;"
Could you, could you, blame them, pray?

II.

Youth, while mantling in the cheek,
Only knows what nature's will is;
Grey-beards' precepts, then, are weak;
Ev'ry Damon has his Phillis.
Nature's law we all confess,
And, when nature points the way,
Tho' Age say " no!" still Youth says " yes!"—
Can you, can you, blame us, pray?

Zouns! here he comes again. If the bumpkin returns before Risk is ready, we are undone.

Enter VIGIL, *and* TOTTERTON, *from the house.*

Vig. Time enough;—'tis but a little after ten, now, I tell you

Tott. But my nephew must have been waiting these two hours. I must make haste, and— (*going*) Eh! why, there's that officer skulking about still.

Beld. Your servant, sir, (*coming forward*) I am still here, you see;—but don't be alarm'd.

Vig. Oh no;—ha, ha! I'm not so easily frighten'd.

Beld. I couldn't leave the field, without paying all due homage to the conqueror.

Vig. Ha!—Then I have no longer the honour, I suppose, of talking to Mr. Kaiserman.

Beld. No, sir;—you are talking to Frederick Beldare, Captain of Grenadiers, and nephew to General Thunder.

Vig. Why, sir, you have render'd me famous, and secure, for ever. Nobody, now, will dare to attack the man, who has defeated the brave Frederick Beldare, Captain of Grenadiers, and nephew to General Thunder.

Beld. (*aside*) Oh, curse your sneering! Why, where can Risk be, all this time? (RISK *appears*) Oh, yonder he goes. You say right Mr. Vigil;

[RISK *slinks from the hotel, dress'd as* SOLO-MON LOB, *and goes to the back of the scene.*]
I'll never measure swords again with an enemy, so much my superior in knowledge;—and thus I quit the field of battle.

[*Exit, into the hotel.*
Vig. And that's the last I hope to see of the bold nephew of the great General Thunder.

FINALE.

RISK, coming forward as SOLOMON LOB, and bowing to VIGIL and TOTTERTON.

Your pardon, good gentlefolks, pray;
I am strange-like, in Lunnun, and I shou'd be
glad,
If you'd just be so kind, to a poor country lad,
As to larn un to find out his way.

Beldare. (at the balcony of the hotel.)
I'll listen.
Vigil. .... *Friend*—
Risk. .... *Ees*—
Vigil. .... *Let me know*
The street to which you want to go.

Risk. (giving a letter.)
This letter, sir, will sartify.

Vigil (reading.)
" *To Mr. Vigil.*"—'*Sbud! 'tis I.*
Risk. *What, you!*
Vigil. *Yes, I*

Risk.   *Wauns! here's a frisk!*
Tott.   *Why, here's a frisk!*
Risk.   *Wauns! here's a frisk!*
       Beldare. (at the balcony.)
     Oh! bravo, bravo, Risk!
     [VIGIL, here, opens and reads the letter.
Tott. *Solomon Lob, or I'm mistaken.*
Risk. *That's I, as sure as bacon's bacon.*
Tott. *Why, nephew!*
Risk. .... *Uncle!*
Both. .... *Is it you!*
Risk. *Ees.*
Tott.   *Yes.*
Both. *Lord, love you, how d'ye do ?* (they embrace.)
       Vigil. (after reading letter.)
   The Parson's letter's right ,—but where
   Is all the money that he sends ?
       Risk. (giving him the purse.)
   Here, sir ;—and uncle, mother, there,
   Has sent you news of all our friends.
           (gives TOTTERTON a letter.)
       Beldare and Risk. (aside.)
   The gudgeons bite already ;
   They swallow every lie.
       Vigil and Totterton.
   An honest lad, and steady ;
   I'll $\begin{Bmatrix} count \\ read \end{Bmatrix}$ *it by and bye.*

SOLOMON LOB, enters at the the back of the
               Stage.

Lob.   *I ha' got my portmantle again,*
    By gum, without any resistance.
Beld. *Confusion! we're ruin'd, that's plain ;*
    For the bumpkin appears at a distance.
   This way! this way! (beckoning Solomon.)
Lob.   *Ees, I'll come.*
   I knows the house ;—I'se not a dunce.
     (RISK, here, observes BELD. and LOB.)
Risk. *Uncle, sha'n't us now go home ?*
       Vigil and Totterton.
   Yes, my lad, come in, at once.
     [SOLOMON LOB goes into the hotel, to
      which BELDARE has beckon'd him.]

Beldare and Risk.

Huzza! we're in safety once more!
Our triumph will soon be complete.

Vigil and Totterton.

Come in, my lad, this is the door;
We have talk'd long enough in the street.

(to RISK.)

Follow us ;—we'll lead the way.

Risk. *Ees, I'll come.*
Beld.   *Huzza! huzza!.*

[VIGIL and TOTTERTON take RISK, as
the supposed SOLOMON LOB, into
VIGIL's house.]

END OF ACT I.

ACT II.

SCENE I.—Vigil's *Painting-room*.

A large window, in the back scene;—the bottom part of which is shaded by a green curtain. Busts, and pictures, in different parts of the room;—some finish'd, some unfinish'd. Among the rest, a picture, on an easel, in an unfinish'd state, representing figures as large as life. A table, with large port-folios on it. A marble slab, on a pedestal, to grind colours.

Enter Vigil, *and* Lydia.

Lyd. I shall not sit as a model for any of your pictures, to day, sir.

Vig. Now, was ever any thing so perverse! Why, Lydia,—why do you always take such a pleasure in thwarting my wishes?

Lyd. Only as a suitable return, sir, for your always thwarting mine.

Vig. You are to remember, madam, that I have taken upon myself the care of your conduct, and education.

Lyd. That's as much as to say, you have taken upon yourself the privilege of tormenting me, from morning to night.

Vig. And dare you tell me, to my face, that—

Lyd. Sir, I dare tell you that the death of my father should make me free; that, in confiding me to the affectionate care of your sister, whose memory I shall always cherish, he never meant to expose me to your tyranny;—in one word, that immuring me here, as your slave, is usurping the rights of nature, and abusing one of the most sacred trusts.—And, now, sir, as you have often complain'd of my giddiness, (*laughing*) you see I have been serious, for the first time.

Vig. Charming spirits you are in, to-day, indeed!—and the best receipt for high spirits, I perceive, is a love-letter, dangling at the end of a parcel of ribbands.

Lyd. What do you mean?

Vig. It as come to hand;—but not exactly as you intended.—(*taking it from his pocket and unfolding it*) Here it is.

Lyd. (*endeavouring to take it from him*)—Dear!—I can't conceive how you——

Vig. How I came by it:—but nothing escapes me, you see.

Lyd. (*smiling*) Then it seems you have got my letter.

Vig. And pray, good madam, how will you clear up this subject, to me?

Lyd. Very easily.—Here's the answer to it.
(*shewing* BELDARE'S *letter.*)

Vig. The answer!—(*attempting to snatch it.*)

Lyd. Softly, sir;—softly, if you please:—you treasure *your* letter, and I *mine*, you know.—(*reads*) " I am call'd Frederick Beldare;—a " Captain of Grenadiers, nephew of a gallant " General.—My love for you is most ardent, and " I swear to unite my destiny to your's."—Now, that's open and honourable; isn't it, sir?

Vig. (*looking over and reading*) " I cannot " explain myself further;—as I write this ab-" solutely in the presence of your Argus."—Zouns! in my presence!—When?—where? how?

Lyd. (*reading*) " In the open street, behind " his back, but close at his elbow."

Vig. Oh, the devil !

Lyd. " And this, I trust, will not be the only " time I shall make a fool of him."—Then you were by ?—on the very spot !

Vig. Yes, yes—damn it, I was sure enough !
                                        (*goes to his painting.*)

Lyd. Ha ! ha ! ha !—I am positively in love with him, for his cleverness :—and I dare say he is very handsome.

Vig. Lydia, I——

Lyd. Come—you are famous for catching a likeness ; and as you have the brush in your hand, do, now, paint me his picture.

Vig. (*throwing the brush away*) Confound the brush, Beldare, pen, ink, paper, and all ribband weavers !

Enter TOTTERTON, *and* RISK.—RISK *carrying* SOLO-MON LOB's *cloak bag.*

Tott. Put it down there, my boy ;—under that table.

     [RISK *puts down the bag, and affects ex-treme awkwardness.*]

Lyd. So !—this is the precious nephew we have so long expected !

Risk. Aye, madam !—I's Solomon Lob ;—you'll find me varry handy about t' house. When I was at whoam i't' country, I always help'd mother to make her hog's puddings.

Tott. The lad has talents.

Risk. Zo I be comed fra Tadcaster, to look a'ter you ; and to mind measter's orders, there, madam.   (*pointing to* VIGIL, *who is painting.*)

Vig. That's a good lad.—Always mind my orders.

Lyd. Not content, then, with your own and Totterton's teasing, I am to have the additional plague of being watch'd by this booby.

Risk. Booby !—wauns ! madam, you'll find I another guess sort of a person from what you do think, only mind my words.—If I could but whisper a single sentence !　　　　(*aside.*)

Vigil. (*painting*) Totterton.

Tott. Sir.

Vigil. I want some black.

Tott. I'll grind it, directly.

Risk I'll do't for ye, mun.

> [*crossing towards* LYDIA, *who is re-perusing the letter from* BELDARE. *He coughs and makes signs to her : she remains with her eyes fix'd on the letter.*]

Vigil. (*to* TOTT.) Where's Sampson Thwack, the bruiser, to-day, that he doesn't come to me, as a model ?

Tott. Sick, in bed ;—he was up late, last night, at the Cat and Bagpipes.

Vigil. A drunken rascal !

Lyd. (*taking her eyes from the letter, and observing* RISK) Why, I declare this blockhead is winking at me !

Vigil. What ! (*starting up.*)

Tott. Mercy on us ! Why Solomon ! are you mad ?

Risk. (*rubbing his eye*) E'en a'most, fegs ! —A plaguy gnat ha' gotten i' my left eye, and nigh blinded me.

Tott. Oh, was that it !

Vigil. Ha, ha ! poor fellow !—No, no, he doesn't look like one of the winking sort, not he. (*to* TOTTERTON). Then, I have no hopes of seeing Thwack, to-day ?

Tott. No.

Vigil. The scoundrel has got drunk on purpose to vex me.—Two hours sitting would be

E

enough;—and the picture must be shipp'd for Russia this evening. You too, madam Lydia,—I'm obliged to you for it,—won't let me take advantage of your features to finish my work.—Zouns! I believe the whole world conspires to smother my efforts, and ruin me in my profession.

[*He deranges his painting apparatus, peevishly, and throws himself into an arm chair.—During this,* TOTTERTON *has taken* RISK *to the marble, on which the colours are placed, and appears teaching him to grind them.*]

Lyd. Come,—you shan't say I have hurt you in your profession.—I *will* sit to you.

Vig. Will you?—Come now, that's kind.

Lyd. But, remember, 'tis on one condition.

Vig. And what's that?

Tott. (*to* RISK, *who is grinding colours, and, at the same time, watching* LYDIA.) There, work away, and I'll be with you again, presently. [*Exit.*

Lyd. Why, the condition is,—that I go to the Exhibition, to-morrow.

Vig. What, to meet that infernal Captain of Grenadiers?—Zouns, madam, and do you think I'll be such a dupe?

Lyd. Just as you please.—No Exhibition, for me, to-morrow,—no sitting, for you, to-day; that's all.

Vig. And have you the assurance to——

Lyd. Oh, if you are getting into a passion, I shall retire to my chamber. (*going.*)

Vig. Nay, but, Lydia——

LYDIA, *singing*.

A Guardian there was, and a crab was he;
  Fal, de ral, de ral, lal, la.—
He kept his Ward under lock and key;
  Fal, de ral, de ral, lal, la.
He tried to plague her, all the day;
But she danced and sang the hours away.
    Fal, lal, lal, &c.

II.

She laugh'd at this crab, as long as she could;
  Fal, de ral, de lal, lal, la.
For fretting never does us good;
  Fal, de ral, de ral, lal, la.
But he grew more teasing every day;
So she took to her heels, and ran away.
    Fal, lal, lal, &c.

                                [Exit.

Vigil. Nay—Lydia—Lydia!—
                      [Exit, following her.
  Risk. (*coming from the marble slab*) So!—
the sly hound has lost the scent.—Now, to see
if my master is watching, at the back of the
house.—(*goes to the window, lifts up the green
curtain, and peeps out*). No—not come, yet.—
How deuced pretty Vigil's ward is!—but, a
little wild devil, she had near discover'd me to
the Guardian.—That stupid dotard, Totterton,
too, asks me so many questions about Tadcaster, and his family, that——Stay,—he's within
hearing, for he's toddling in and out every minute.—I'll bawl out a Yorkshire ditty, that
shall split the old fellow's ears.—

    *[Goes to the marble slab, and sings, while he
      is grinding the colours.]*

SONG.—RISK.

TUNE.—"Ally Croker."

*A Captain, bold, in Halifax, that dwelt in country
    quarters,*
*Seduced a maid, who hang'd herself, one morning, in
    her garters;*
*His wicked conscience smited him; he lost his stomach,
    daily;*
*He took to drinking ratifia, and thought upon Miss
    Bailey.*
    Oh, Miss Bailey! unfortunate Miss Bailey!

II.

*One night, betimes, he went to rest, for he had caught
    a fever;*
*Says he, " I am a handsome man, but I'm a gay de-
    ceiver."*
*His candle, just at twelve o'clock, began to burn quite
    palely;*
*A ghost stepp'd up to his bed-side, and said, " behold
    Miss Bailey!"*
        Oh! Miss Bailey! &c.

III.

*" Avaunt, Miss Bailey!" then he cried, " your face
    looks white, and mealy!"*
*" Dear Captain Smith," the ghost replied, " you've
    used me ungenteelly.*
*" The Crowner's 'quest goes hard with me, because
    I've acted frailly,*
*" And Parson Biggs won't bury me, though I am
    dead Miss Bailey."*
        Oh! Miss Bailey! &c.

IV.

*" Dear corpse," says he, " since you and I, accounts
    must, once for all, close,*
*" I've got a one-pound note, in my regimental small-
    clothes;*
*" 'Twill bribe the Sexton for your grave;"—the ghost,
    then, vanish'd, gaily,*
*Crying, " bless you, wicked Captain Smith! remem-
    ber poor Miss Bailey."*
        Oh! Miss Bailey! &c.

Enter TOTTERTON, *with a box of colours.*

Tott. Adsbobs! well sung!—I didn't think, boy, you had such a voice.

Risk. Clerk of our parish larn'd I to chaunt, wi' his pitch-fork.

Tott. What, old Davy Drone, of Tadcaster?

Risk. Ees.

Tott. Aha!—why he's one of my oldest friends. —And how is he?

Risk. Oh, zouns! I must kill all his old friends, or he'll ask questions about 'em, for ever. (*aside*) He be dead.

Tott. Davy Drone dead?—bless us!—and your mother not to write me word!—Ah!—— he must have been old!—I think about—— Didn't he die at eighty-four?

Risk. Noa;—at five in the morning.

Tott. Umph!—And honest Mat Figgins, the grocer,—is he hale, and hearty?

Risk. He be dead, too.

Tott. He dead too!—Poor Mat!—his lump-sugar was excellent!—he had a dog, I remember, that chuck'd a halfpenny off his nose, into his mouth, whenever you said nine.—Is the dog alive?

Risk. Noa;—he eat a halfpenny.

Tott. And, did that kill him?

Risk. Ees;—'tware such a very bad one.

Tott. Well, and what's become of old Gruntlepool, the undertaker?

Risk. He's gone dead too; and were buried last Christmas.

Tott. What the death-hunter dead, too!— Why, bless us, they do nothing but die, at Tadcaster! what's the reason of it, Solomon?—

Risk. We ha' gotten three more pottycaries.

Tott. Oh, then, I don't wonder.—But, come, 'tis almost dinner time. Make haste, and grind out the black, and then for the shoulder of mutton. (*going*) Dear, dear, fifty years ago, who'd have thought my old friends would have dropt off so fast !   (*goes out.*)

Risk. Oh, curse your questions! my master must have waited in the street till he's out of all patience.—They seem all busy, for a moment, at least ;—so I'll untie the ladder of ropes, that I have cramm'd into honest Solomon Lob's cloak bag. (*untying it*) Without this ladder of ropes we could have done nothing.

Re-Enter TOTTERTON.

Tott. (*seeing him busied with the cloak-bag*) Ah !—that cloak bag's the very thing I came for. —I had forgot to take it into the hall; Mr. Vigil can't abide a litter. (*takes it from him.*)

Risk. (*uneasy*) Noa, uncle, noa ;—I'll take it into the hall.

Tott. Tut, boy ! 'tisn't heavy.—

Risk. Odrabbit it, there be a deal more in't than you do think for.

Enter VIGIL.

Vig. Totterton.

Tott. Eh?

Vig. Come here.—

    [TOTTERTON *goes with him to the front of the stage, having put down the cloak-bag.—* RISK *returns to the marble slab.*]

Lydia will sit for the picture, provided I take her to the Exhibition, to-morrow.

Tott. Don't do it.

Vig. Hold your tongue; I've promised her.

Tott. She'll give you the slip there.—Mind, 'twas I said so.

Vig. Pshaw!—you're an old blockhead.—She's coming to the painting room, here, directly;—dress'd for the subject I'm painting.

Tott. And what will you do for Sampson Thwack?—who's to stand up for him?

Vig. Why, I told Lydia I had a great mind to try Solomon Lob;—but she won't hear of it.—Between ourselves, she's right; for I must say, though he's your nephew, he's the awkwardest rascal I ever saw in my life. (*taking* TOTTERTON *farther from* RISK.) Come more this way;—a thought has struck me.—

> [*During the following conversation,* RISK *steals to the cloak-bag, which he opens, and shuts; after having taken out a ladder of ropes, which he hides under several portfolios, placed on the table.*]

There's a barrack not far off.

Tott. I know it.

Vig. Couldn't you get me a soldier, off duty?—only for a couple of hours.

Tott. To be sure I can.

Vig. Tell him I'll pay him handsomely:—and harkee,—pick out a strong, well-made fellow;—as like Thwack as you can.

Tott. I will.   (*going.*)

Vig. And, stay;—be sure he's one of your own chusing.—Bring him here yourself, else, some dangerous designing dog may get into the house, and——

Tott. Oh, let me alone.   (*going.*)

Risk. (*who is now return'd to the slab*) Dost'e want me to gang and help you wi' ony thing, uncle?

Tott. No, no,—stay where you are, boy.
                            [*Exit, with the bag.*

Vig. As for you, Solomon Lob, remember to execute, faithfully, all that I order you.

Risk. I will, sir.

Vig. If Miss Lydia desires you to carry a letter, bring it to me, directly.

Risk. I will, sir.

Vig. You are to watch her at every turn, you know.

Risk. Ees—that's what I be come'd here for, sir.

Vig. (*taking his palette, and returning again to his work*) At last, then, I shall finish my picture.—A charming subject!—Cressida giving her glove to Troilus, on his quitting Troy, for the Grecian Camp.

Enter LYDIA.

Risk. Now, if I could but make her know me!   (*aside.*)

Vig. (*to* LYDIA) Well, Lydia!—why how comes it you are not dress'd, for the subject I am painting?

Lyd. We must have a word or two of explanation, yet, before we finish our treaty.

Vig. Pshaw!—what's the matter, now?

Lyd. Imprimis;—you are to take me to the Exhibition.

Vig. Granted.

Lyd. But we are not to sneak in, remember, after dinner, when all the company is gone. The middle of the day, and a full room; that's my stipulation.

Vig. Well, I——well, come, that's granted, too.

Lyd. Very well, then;—when you have perform'd your promise, I'll perform mine.

Vig. Why, zouns! you must sit directly. Won't you take my word, 'till to-morrow?

TRIO.

LYDIA, VIGIL, and RISK.

LYDIA.

No, no ;—I doubt you much, I vow, sir ;
Your promises are mighty fine ;—
Give me the Exhibition, now, sir ;
Allons! we'll to't before we dine.

VIGIL. (sneering.)
Your Captain, in the throng,
Waits there, his love to meet.

RISK. (aside, and pointing to the window.)
Upon my soul, you're wrong,
He's waiting in the street.

LYDIA.
Excuse me, sir, your word I doubt :
I'll tell you how it comes about ;—
Deceit has always been your plan.

VIGIL.
'Zouns! madam, do you mean to flout ?
You fret me worse than law, or gout,
Or all the plagues that pester man!

RISK. (aside.)
How shall I make her find me out ?
How tell her I am not the lout ?
I must inform her if I can.

LYDIA.
Well, no more words,—since words are galling.

RISK. (singing clownishly, and grinding the colours.)
Tol, lol, loddy, loddy do.

VIGIL.
Why, how that awkward booby's bawling!

LYDIA. (going away.)
What's said, is said, and past recalling.

VIGIL. (peevishly.)
Well, no more words.

RISK. (aside.)
She must not go.

F

VIGIL and LYDIA.
What's said, is said, and past recalling.

RISK. (still grinding, and repeating the burden of the
Couplets, in the first Act.)

" *He who pities maids, like thee,*
" *Hither comes to set you free.*"

LYDIA. (who stops, suddenly, on hearing RISK; she
looks stedfastly at him, without being per-
ceived by VIGIL, who has, at this moment, turn'd his back, and is occupied
with his painting.)

Hark! heard I right!—that air I know!—

VIGIL. (seeing LYDIA return.)
Why, Lydia, will you plague me daily?
Why will you vex your guardian so?

RISK. (still grinding.).
" *Oh, Miss Bailey! unfortunate Miss Bailey!*"

LYDIA. (hiding her agitation, and at times looking
towards RISK.)
Come, I relent;—I might be wrong:
I'll sit:—good nature is my vice.

RISK. (aside.)
She caught the burden of the song,
By jingo, in a trice!

LYDIA.
Good humour now prevailing,
  Let all our bickerings cease;—
Adieu, to spleen and railing!
  Our quarrel ends in peace.
VIGIL.
Good humour, &c.
RISK.
My lucky stars prevailing;
  My hopes, how they increase!
I've now, no fear of failing!
  The prisoner I'll release.

} together

Lyd. Since the man is ill, sir, who was to sit for this picture, to-day,—suppose we—— hem——suppose we try Totterton's nephew, here. (*pointing to* RISK) He's quite a simpleton, to be sure;—but perhaps he may answer the purpose.

Risk. Did you want I, madam? (*whispering her*) I am Captain Beldare's man.

Lyd. Yes;—now I look at him again, I think he'll answer the purpose, very well.

Vig. Why, you told me, in the room, just now, he look'd like a goose.

Lyd. Certainly, at first sight, I——but, poor fellow, he seems very anxious to be of service.

Risk. That's what I do, madam.—Odrabbit it! sir, miss do see what I be good for, better nor you.

Vig. Pshaw!—nonsense!—I've sent for a soldier.

Lyd. A soldier!

Vig. I expect him, here, every minute.

Lyd. Oh, very well;—I'll run, and get on my dress;—but you have lock'd it up;—I can't get it without the key of the gallery.

Vig. Well, well, I—— (*hesitating*)—— Well, come, here it is. (*gives her the key.*)

Lyd. (*aside, and going*) A soldier!—and Beldare's man here.—This means something,— and time will explain it. [*Exit.*

Vig. She has made it up so soon, that I am mistaken if she hasn't some mischief in her head.—And I, too, to be such a blockhead, to trust her with the key of that gallery!—I'll lay my life she's peeping out there, to give Beldare some clue to find her, at the Exhibition, to-morrow.—I'll be after her, directly.

F 2

(*going*)

Enter TOTTERTON, *and a* GRENADIER.

Tott. Here, I have brought you a thumper.

Vig. (*looking at the grenadier*) Aye—well—I—yes.—Put him into the dress;—I'll be here in a minute.   (*runs out.*)

Tott. Bless my soul!—he has shot off like a piece of quicksilver!—where is he going in such a hurry!—

Gren. Come, old one,—be alive; I've no time to spare.

Tott. (*taking a breast-plate from an arm'd chair*) Well, patience, patience.—You are off duty, you know, honest friend.

Gren. We have a roll-call at five; I musn't be too late.

Tott. Time enough, time enough.—And what is your name, friend?

Gren. Dub.

Tott. Dub!—bless me! that's a very short name, for a grenadier!—come, put by your cap.

Gren. (*putting the cap on the chair*) But, I say, my hearty,—besides the half crown, you know, I'm to have a pot of porter for a compliment.

Tott. Aye, aye—we shan't quarrel about that.—Come you, and help us. (*to* RISK)—Here's the breast-plate, and (*taking it up; the breast-plate.*)   (*bell rings.*)
Hark! that's my master's bell!—there's the helmet and beard, and (*bell rings again*)—Coming! coming!—help the honest man, Solomon.   [*Exit.*

Risk. Ees, uncle, I will.

Gren. Is that old buck your uncle?

Risk. Now's my time, or never !

> [RISK *quits the* GRENADIER, *whose arms are pass'd half way through the arm-holes of the breast-plate, and runs to the rope-ladder, which he has hid under the port-folios.*]

Gren. Why, what the devil do you leave me hand-cuff'd so for ?

Risk. (*opening the window, and throwing out the rope ladder, which he fixes to the balcony.*) Quick ! quick !—come up !—leave your cloak in the street.

Gren. (*disentangles himself from the breast-plate, and throws it on the floor*) Zouns !—they have brought me into this house to rob me.—

> [*Draws his sword, and stands on his guard.* BELDARE, *at the same time, appears at the window, and jumps into the room.*]

Gren. Why, 'tis my own Captain !

Beld. Ha !—*you* here, my lad !—how came you into this house ?   (*to the Grenadier.*)

Risk. To help gallantry, and relieve beauty, sir.

Gren. Beauty, you ugly dog ! what do you mean ?

Risk. (*rapidly*) Get down that ladder as quick as you can ;—take my master's cloak, that you'll find at the bottom of it.—Wait for me at the publick-house, at the corner :—I'll be with you in a quarter of an hour, and you shall drink your skin-full, to the health of Captain Beldare.

Beld. Do so, my lad ;—and I'll reward you handsomely, depend on't.

Gren. Quick march, then !—(*goes to take up his cap and sword.*)

Risk. No, no ;—leave your cap and sword ; we shall want them.

Gren. Leave my accoutrements !—Captain ?

(hesitating.)

Beld. I'll be answerable for them.

Gren. Well, Captain, if any thing should come on't, you'll bear me harmless. Pray take care of my sword, Captain ;—it stuck by me all last war, and somehow, I have a love for it.

(getting out at the window.)

Beld. I'll be careful of it. I enter into your sentiments, my brave fellow ! a British soldier always feels an affection for the weapon he has used, against the enemies of old England.

[*The* GRENADIER *goes down the ladder, and* RISK *shuts the window.*]

Risk. Now, sir, your hat, if you please,—and on with this helmet and breast-plate, immediately.

Beld. Explain all in two words, before any body comes.—

(Gives RISK *his hat, who hides it behind the port-folios.)*

Risk. In two words, then,—you are the grenadier that is just gone out at window ;—and, over and above the money for your trouble, you'll get a pot of porter.

Beld. What for ?

Risk. For coming as a model to old Vigil, for one of his pictures.

Beld. I conceive.—*(during this,* RISK *is dressing* BELDARE) Is Lydia handsome ?

Risk. As an angel !

Beld. As I predicted !—I won't quit the house without her.

Risk. Softly, sir, softly !—we shall be discover'd.

Beld. That's true ;—but how am I to hide my face ?

Risk. Here's a wig and beard, sir, which belong to the dress;—they will disguise it, I warrant. And now, I think, we——(*tries it on*) ha! here's somebody coming!

Enter TOTTERTON.

Tott. Why, there's a young man at the door, says he is my nephew, Solomon Lob.

Risk. (*aside*) Zouns! we're discover'd!—Why uncle, you don't say so?

Tott. Sure as you are there;—but he don't bamboozle me.—What do you think?

Risk. What!

Tott. I saw him stealing from the hotel over the way,—where that officer lives.

Risk. Did you, by gum!

Tott. Yes;—a rogue the Captain has hired to carry on his plots.

Risk. Wauns! uncle, you ha' hit on't.

Tott. Oh, let me alone for finding out a cheat. He won't go from the door,—so there let him stay.—Well, have you dress'd the—— (*looking at* BELDARE) Aye,—very well;—the helmet a little more up,—there.— (*arranging the dress*) An impudent knave!—to think to impose upon me!

Enter VIGIL.

Vig. I've got my keys again, and she is safe.—Oh, this is the man for the model.

Tott. Much about the size of Thwack; isn't he?

Vig. (*taking* TOTTERTON *aside*) But are you quite sure he's a soldier?

Tott. Pugh!—I brought him from the barracks, myself.

Vig. Enough.—And how much money are you to have, my lad?   (BELDARE *pauses.*)

Tott. He's to have half a crown.

Beld. And a pot of porter.—

Vig. Aye, aye,—two if you like.—Totterton, see if Lydia's ready.—   [*Exit* TOTTERTON. What regiment do you belong to, my lad?

Beld. The First.

Vig. Indeed!—then, perhaps, you know an officer call'd Beldare, nephew to General Thunder?

Beld. He's my own Captain.

Vig. Is he?—then you may tell him, from me, if he ever hopes to set a foot in this house, he's plaguily mistaken.

Beld. I will.

Enter LYDIA, *dress'd for the picture, preceded by* TOTTERTON.

Lyd. (*aside to* RISK, *as she enters*) Who is that soldier?

Risk. (*aside to* LYDIA) He's my master.

Vig. So, Lydia, you are ready, I see.

Lyd. Is this the soldier, sir, who is to be my companion?

Vig. Yes;—a good subject:—though it seems, madam, he knows your Captain Beldare.

Lyd. Indeed!

Beld. I was in his company, when I received my last wound, madam.

Vig. Wounded, were you?

Lyd. And, how did you get your wound, pray?

Beld. In scaling a fortress, which the enemy thought impregnable. A rich treasure was lock'd up in it. I mounted a ladder, and got into the building through a window;—but I had hardly been five minutes in the place, before I received a deep wound, just——just on this side, madam. (*placing his hand on his left side.*)

Lyd. On——on the side of the heart?

Beld. Yes, madam.

Lyd. But it was very slight, I suppose.

Beld. Oh, no;—very dangerous. I shall feel the effects of it for the rest of my life, madam.

Lyd. For the rest of your life!—poor man! I pity you, sincerely.

Vig. Come, come—we lose time;—let's to business.—You see this picture, friend;—this is the position I want.—Now take that lady's hand; kneel, and look her full in the face.

Beld. (*kneeling, and taking* Lydia's *hand*) The lady, I am afraid, will think me very awkward.

Lyd. Oh, no! not in the least.

Tott. (*who has been busied in various parts of the room*) Bless my soul!—here's a hat with a spanking cockade, cramm'd under the port folios! (*a violent tap is heard at the window.*) Eh?—why, what's that?

[*The* Grenadier *opens the window, and looks in.*]

Gren. I must attend parade, directly. Tell Captain Beldare to chuck me my sword.

Vig. Captain Beldare!

Risk. (*throwing the sword to the* Grenadier) Take your sword, and go to the devil!

(*the* Grenadier *disappears.*)

Vig. Why zouns!—am I betray'd!

Beld. (*throwing off his disguise.*) Even so, sir.—I am that Captain Beldare, who, in spite

G

of your bolts, bars, and locksmiths, cherish'd hopes of setting foot in your house; and have not been, you see, so plaguily mistaken.

Vig. And how the devil did you get in?

Risk. Oh, I let my master in, sir, at that window.

Tott. His master!—Oh! my poor Solomon Lob!   [*runs out.*

Vig. And, now, sir, you have got into my house, do me the favour to go out of it.

Beld. With all my heart, when this lady accompanies me.

Vig. Sir, this lady shall——

Beld. Nay, nay;—no blustering. Look ye, Mr. Vigil, I am young, and independent, and this lady intirely free.

Vig. Free?

Beld. Yes, sir;—the law, I know, gives you no power over her.—Resign her quietly, or dread the consequences.—Come, my old boy, listen to terms, and she shall come and sit, as a model, whenever you please.

Lyd. Oh, certainly.

Enter TOTTERTON, *and* SOLOMON LOB.

Tott. Oh, my poor Solomon!—that I took for a rogue, and shut out of doors!

Sol. Ne'er heed it, uncle; I be in, at last. *(to* VIGIL) I be come, sir, to see that nobody do run away wi' miss.

Vig. Upon my soul, you have taken a very pretty time for it!—Well, well, 'tis in vain to murmur, I see. Captain, you have conquer'd; I submit.

Beld. Well resolved!—And if ever you have another ward, under your care, Mr. Vigil, recollect that it is the happy privilege of this country, that its women, like its men, are always free.

FINALE.

BELDARE.

Cupid inflaming us,
Old men
Are fools, when
They ever talk of taming us.
Life's date is quickly past;
Youth's bloom is fading fast;
Know this ;—
Then seize bliss,
And pleasures while they last.

    CHORUS.—Cupid inflaming us, &c.

LYDIA.

Guardians, wishing to secure us,
Only think, and act, like dolts ;
Let them, as they will, immure us,
Love contrives to burst the bolts.

    CHORUS.—Cupid inflaming us, &c.

VIGIL.

Women all our senses cozen ;
Through a maze of wiles they run.
I can paint them, by the dozen,
But I cannot conquer one.
Cupid inflaming her,
Old men
Are fools, then,
Who ever talk of taming her.

    CHORUS.—Cupid inflaming us, &c.

RISK. (to Vigil.)

When you paint the pretty creatures,
Always place a Captain near ;
Nothing heightens more their features
Than a handsome Grenadier.

CHORUS.

Cupid inflaming them,
Old men
Are fools, when
They ever talk of taming them.

END OF THE FARCE.

Printed by B. Deans, Bartholomew,
Covent Garden.